Drawing Spiders
Volume 1
How to Draw Spiders
For the Beginner

I0505624

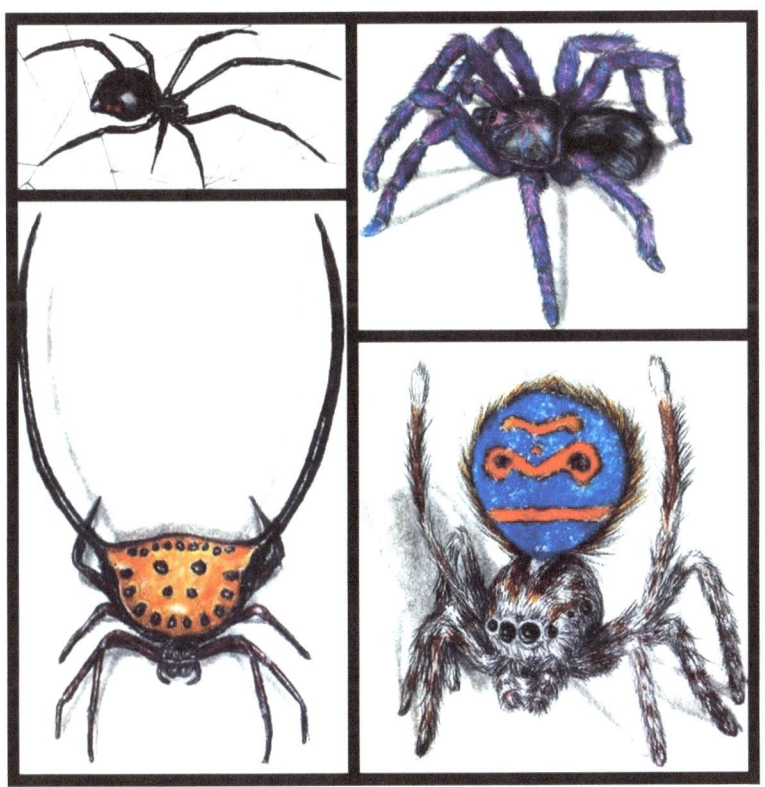

Adrian Sanqui
And
John Davidson

Learn to Draw Series
Mendon Cottage Books
JD- Biz Publishing

All Images Licensed
By: Adrian Sanqui, Paolo Lopez de Leon, Fotolia and 123rf

Learn How to Draw Books for the Absolute Beginner

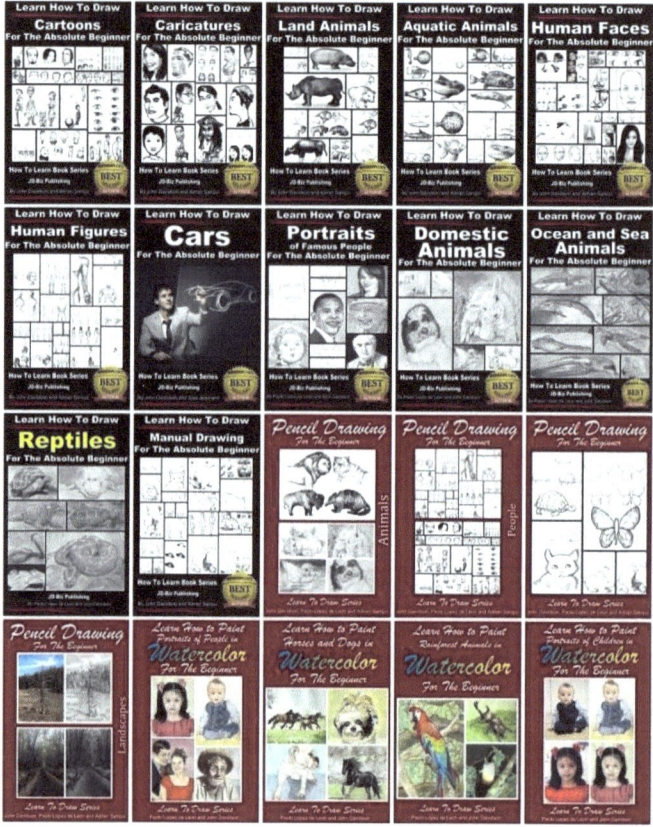

TABLE OF CONTENTS

Drawing tools

Pencils

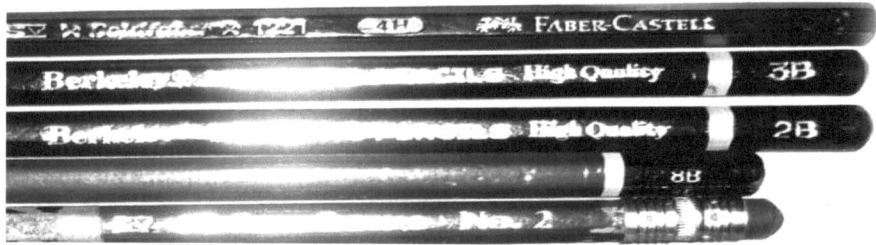

The most important tool you need to be able to enhance your drawing skills is a medium that can be corrected if you made some sloppy line strokes. Knowing and using more than just one type of pencil is a big help and it is better if you have pencils of different grades so you can easily produce the kind of lightness or darkness you want to make. The 'H' engraved near the pencil's tip (side of eraser) stands for "hardness" and it ranges from 2H to 9H. A pencil with only an "H" mark and doesn't have a number means 1H. The most common type (the one available anywhere) of pencil that does not indicate its grade mark is usually a 2H pencil. The "B" marking of pencils stand for "blackness", this means that they can easily produce darker line marks and are softer than H pencils. It ranges from HB (hard and dark) to 9B (very soft and very dark), so when it comes to B pencils, the higher the number is; the softer and darker it becomes. Different brands have different softness, hardness and blackness levels, so if you are going to use a certain brand for the first time, you should try them out first before applying it on your main drawing.

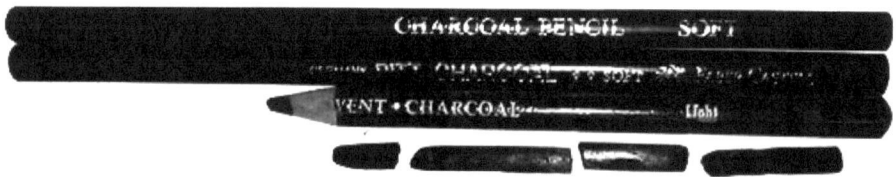

Charcoal pencils also come in different grades. The generic grades of soft, medium and hard are available in different brands. Charcoal pencils are a bit messy to work with; even the 'hard' grade charcoal pencil is still relatively softer compared to those with 4B to 6B grade pencils. It is most advisable for drawings that would require a lot of smeared shading for a smoother and wider portrayal of gradation.

Mechanical
pencil

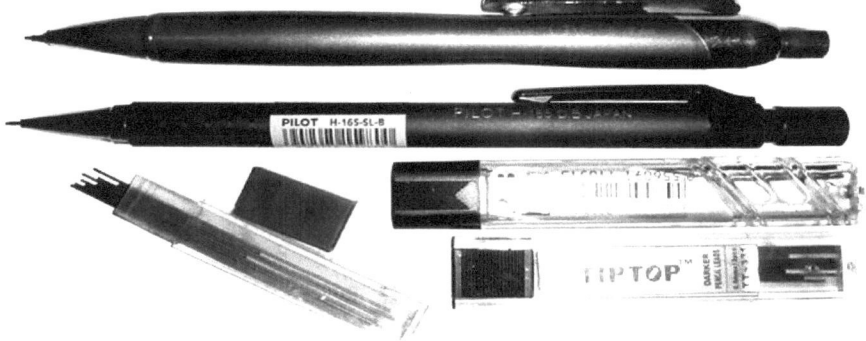

A mechanical pencil has a consistent wick or point which makes it easier for you to maintain the thickness of the line marks you produce. Mechanical pencils are good for small and subtle detailing that requires very thin lines, instead of sharpening your pencil several times just to have a thin and constant fine point that you need. Different grades of lead or graphite is also available for refilling your mechanical pencil, just make sure that the size of the point your pencil has is also the same as the pencil leads you refill it with. They come in several sizes and style, but what really matters is it does what it's supposed to.

Sharpener

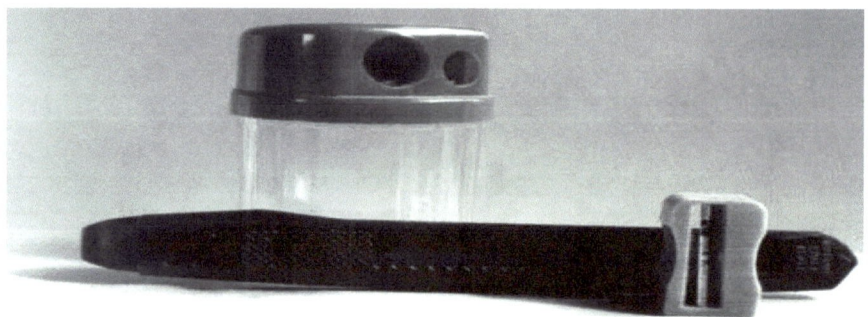

A regular sharpener is quite dependable if you are using H and low B pencils, but if you are going to use it to sharpen a pencil with very soft graphite cores then it may keep on breaking, most especially if you will use it for a charcoal lead pencil. A good substitute for regular sharpeners is a cutter, so you can easily control the pressure that should just be enough to expose the core and achieve a fine point. Cutters are often used if you want a "chisel" point pencil that is very helpful for thick and thin linings.

Erasers

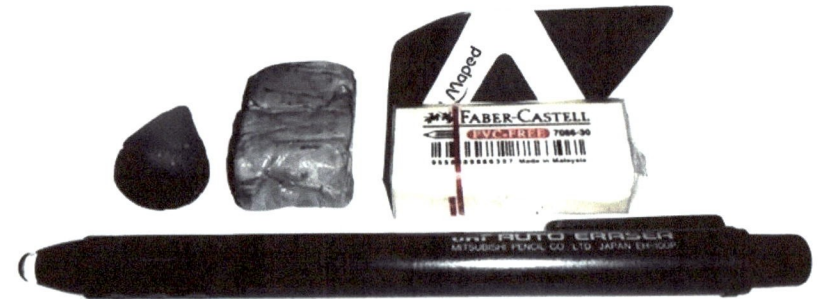

Pencils are no good if you don't have a good quality eraser, having an eraser is essential if you are going to use a pencil for drawing. Choose a rubber eraser that is soft and not the ones that leave a faint color or worst is a scratch on the paper. Don't leave your eraser lying around on the table or just anywhere, keep it on a pencil case or anything that can protect it from being exposed on air for too long because some erasers (cheaper ones) harden when it's left lying around because it will dry out and harden.

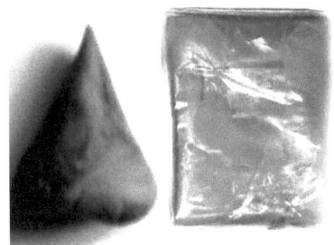

A kneadable eraser is very helpful for making highlights and reaching hardly accessible areas such as the gloss on the eyes or light portions of fingernails and such. It usually looks like a gray slab or a small bar of clay that can be molded or deformed to any shape you desire. It doesn't rub off the marking like usual erasers, but instead, it lifts off the graphite from the paper, like absorbing it. Instead of rubbing the eraser with a certain pressure to remove a marking, carefully dab on the portions you want to erase or to simply decrease the applied graphite or charcoal until you recover the brightness (whiteness of the paper) you want. Kneaded erasers can still be useful as long as they aren't already too dirty or dry. Keep it in a concealed container to lengthen its usefulness, because just like how good it is for absorbing graphite, it would also easily catch dust.

Smudge sticks

A smudge stick is used for smearing the shades on the portions that are hard to access. Some artists dull down the other tip so it can be used for distributing the shades on the big areas. To avoid ruining the smudge stick, use a sand paper to make a blunter tip or to make it even pointier. Smudge sticks or blending stumps comes in different sizes, choose what best fits your needs and it will be a big help for blending gradations. Smudge sticks are cheap and are available on art stores. Common smudge sticks are just rolled and compressed hard papers, so try not to get it wet.

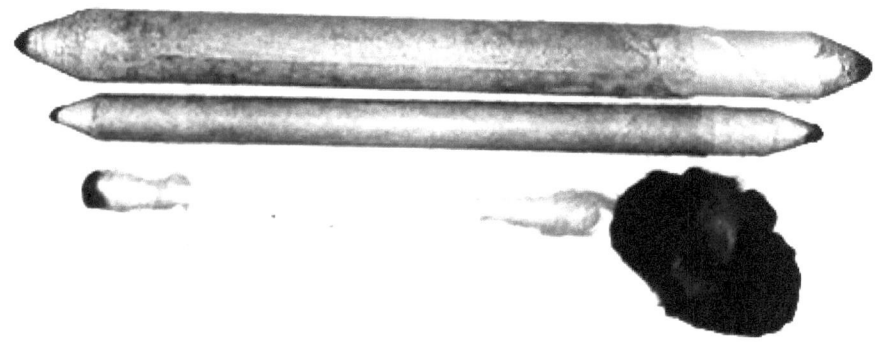

Keep those used up smudge sticks even if it's already in a rugged state (dirty or worn out), you never know when it might get handy. Dirty smudge sticks are useful for producing faint shades, and those with torn up tips can make textures that you might find useful.

If ever you cannot find a smudge stick available (although, I doubt this would be a problem if you have art stores near you, and if not, you can just order online. It is quite cheap) you can just make a tortillion for a temporary smudging tool (some artists actually prefer this one instead of smudge sticks). Use a thick piece of paper (like those on sketch pads, preferably the ones for watercolor drawings. Do not use thin and shiny papers). Fold it on one side and roll it up to create a cone, with the folded side at the tip.

Coloring materials

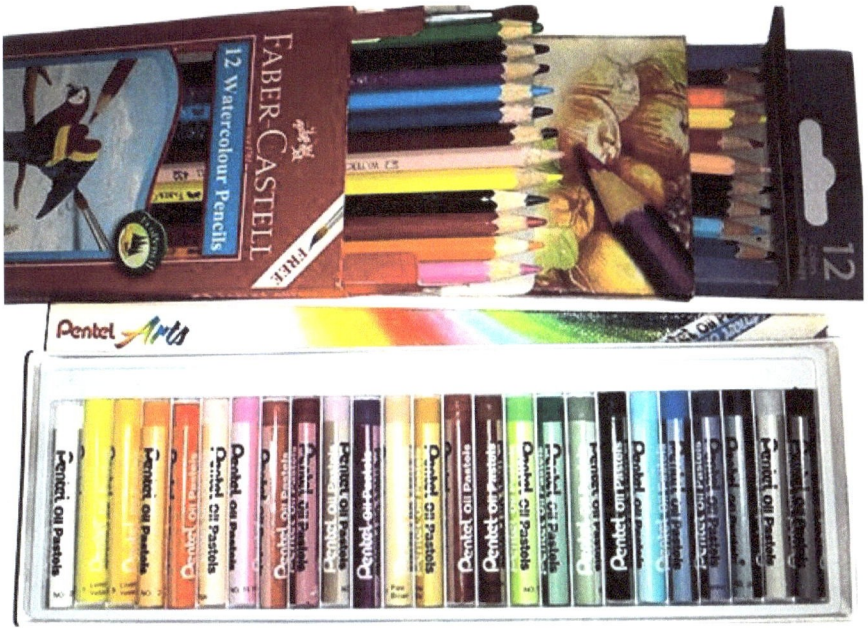

If you are planning to color your drawing, choose a coloring tool that best fits your needs.

Oil pastels are good for blending and synchronizing different colors together. It might get messy on your first trials (if you don't want to get messy, just place a clean piece of paper for your palm rest, to avoid rubbing your palm against the colored portions of your drawing) but you'll get the hang of it as you use it more often. Oil pastels are good for beginners as a practicing tool for smearing different color values.

Color pencils are the next best thing for filling your drawing with colored hatches (linear shading), or even coloring via scribbling. This coloring tool is best for small-sized illustrations. Although, the peak of the tone values that a common color pencil set can produce are far weaker than the oil pastel's, and it cannot be smeared (but there are available color pencils which can produce strong color tones just like oil pastel's or even acrylic's, but they are quite pricy; like the prisma color pencils). This coloring tool is also a good practicing medium for beginners, and my personal favorite for quick colored sketches or even for illustrations with fairly detailed line work.

Parts of a Spider

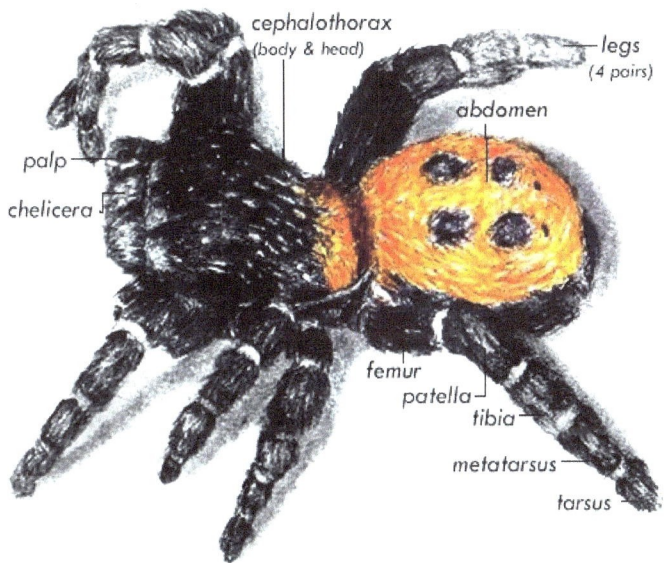

A spider's body structure is divided into two major parts. The upper portion is the cephalothorax (also called prosoma); this includes the spider's head and the thorax. The carapace covers the dorsal side (backside) of the upper body. At the center of the front edge of the head are the palps (the fangs/chelicera are at the lower center of the palps and are usually unnoticable to many species of spiders), and right above the palps are the eyes (number of eyes may differ, either eight or six depending on the breed). The main pair of eyes at the center is usually bigger compared to others. A minor dent/ dimple at the center of the carapace is the fovea, this is usually where the markings of the carapace start (especially on several kinds of tarantulas).

The lower part of the spider's body is its abdomen which is also called opisthosoma. The abdomen is always bigger in size and mass. At the center of the abdomen is the cardiac mark, it may or may not be visible to the other spiders especially those with uniquely shaped abdomens. At the lower edge of the abdomen where the silk comes out is called the spinner, this is barely seen (hidden most of the time) on a spider's dorsal view. Spiders have four pairs of legs (8 in total), and all are connected ventrally (underside) to the prosoma. A spider's leg is composed of 7 segments; the coxa which is connected to the base/upper body, followed by the trochanter which connects the coxa to the femur (the thickest and is usually the longest segment of the leg), then the joint which is the spider's knee called patella, followed by the tibia, metatarsus, and the tarsus which is the leg's tip.

Peacock Spider

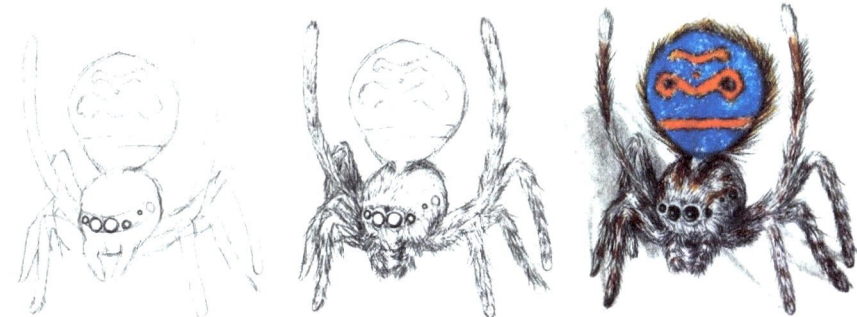

There are a many colorful spiders, but the peacock spider is probably one of the most colorful and fashionable kind, not just on their order of family species, but to the entire family of spiders in general. Or if they are not (one of the most colorful kinds), a few of them will be, because being as colorful and as groovy as they could be are their means of survival. Peacock spiders, also known as gliding spiders or the maratus volans, is a small type of spider that uses its stunning colors to attract their potential mate (female).

The abdomen of a peacock spider is covered in an artistic combination of different colors. It contains a feature that seems like extending flaps wrapped around it, which could extend to form a disk-shaped colorful embellishment or insignia. This unique feature which has a variety of appearance from one to another is used by male peacock spiders to impress or court female peacock spiders that they choose to mate with. The male raises its abdomen, then spread and brag its colors to the female. And in addition to this, it dances (yes, it actually dances, not just by wobbling randomly, but also with a certain beat and patterned jiggling steps). In combination to its raised abdomen displaying its colors, it sticks a pair of its limb and clap with the beat of its groove.

The embellishment on a peacock spider's abdomen varies in different styles and colors. From red, green, yellow, blue, orange, purple, of different shade values. This significant coloration is arranged in different kinds of pattern, and few others containing an iridescent characteristic. Its body is partially covered in short white fur coating, with a portion of red to brown furs on its limbs and head (which usually is in stripes or the color of the entire head) with few stripes of black (which compliments the white and red fur). Its eyes contain an iridescent color of blue and green.

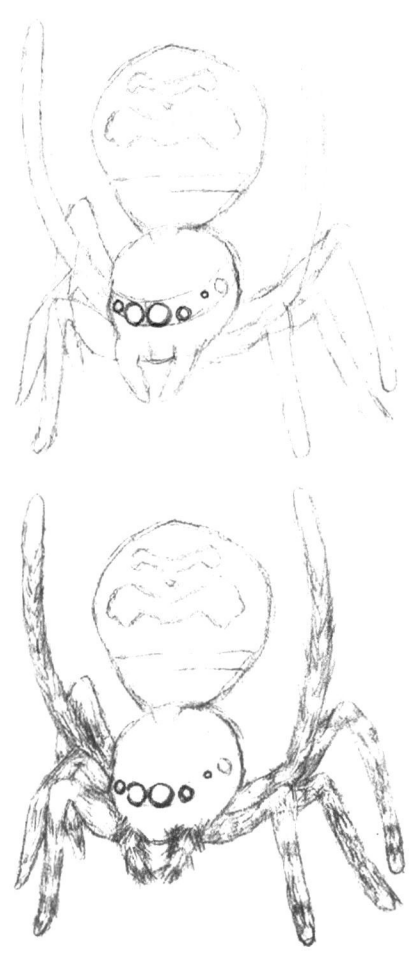

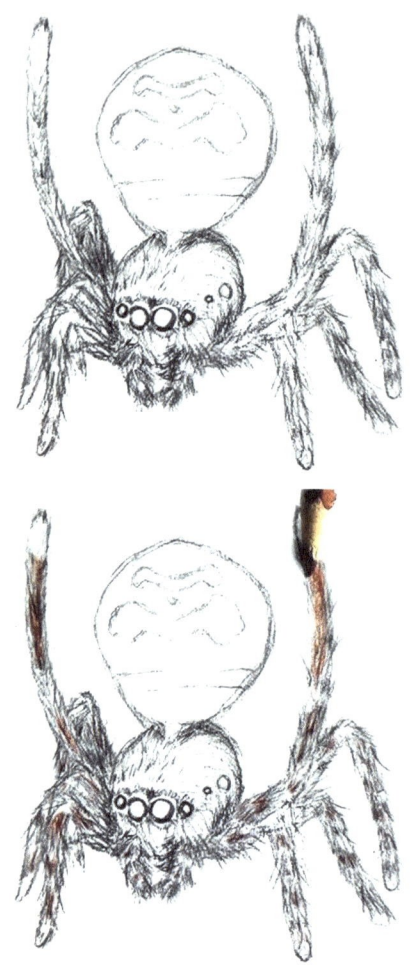

- Begin with the shape outline.

Start with the spherical head of the peacock spider. Draw some lines across the sphere to create a reference line for properly placing the head features (eyes and palps).

Establish the length and thickness of the limbs. You can start with one line per limb to easily convey each of its folds and position. And then define the entire shape of the limbs including the portions overlapped by the other limb next to it. In this way, it is much easier to see if the length and position of each leg are correct, and if they are folded or stretched properly.

- Begin portraying the fur.

The body of a peacock spider is covered in thin short fur and there's hardly a pattern that can be followed (if not for the subtle brown color). Conveying the fur should be done with more than one layer of texture contour.

Make a stripe on the legs with several rows of short contour hatches. Start with short thin lines spiking downward from the surface (area it covers) if the leg is positioned downward, and short lines spiking upwards for the raised pair of limbs. Do the same thing on the palps but the lines should spike wider.

Cover the head with the same kind of short line strokes. The lines should flow or bend with the head's spherical contour shape.

Thicken the fur coating by applying another layer of short contour hatches. This time, make some few short lines that are slightly thicker than the first ones. Add some more wild strands of fur spiking outwards from the legs. At this point, the stripe pattern you made on the limbs should be barely noticeable.

- Apply the brownish color value of the body.

Depict the dark-brown color of the body. Apply the color in the same manner you applied the furry texture. Create few short lines of brown following the stripe pattern of the limbs you previously diminished (do not extend the line strokes outside of the base).

The raised pair of limbs is browner in tone compared to the other limbs, but do not color this portion with long thick line strokes. Make a tight layer of short line strokes on the farther segments of the limb (from the tibia to metatarsus of the legs' segments), with the ends of each row overlapping the next one.

- Thicken the fur.

Once the subtle brown value of the body is conveyed, apply another layer of contour hatches one last time. Put some darker lines striking upwards on the brown area of the raised limbs. Darken the portions that should appear darker (using thicker and darker contour hatches), such as the lower areas of the head (on the sides and the portion beneath the palps) and the lower and farther portions of the limbs.

- Apply the stripes on the head.

The top of the head contains diagonal line marks, having a brighter value of brown (brownish-orange). This color value can be obtained by overlapping some thin lines of brown layer with an orange color.

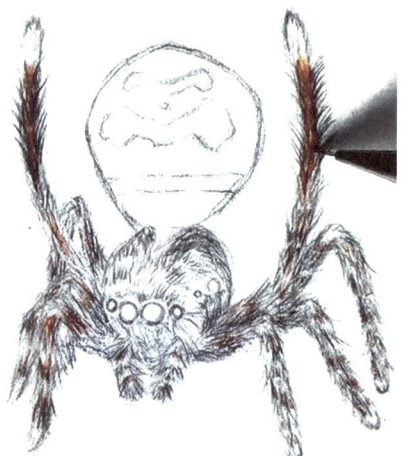

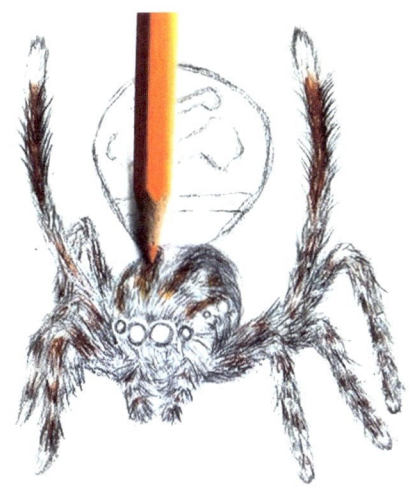

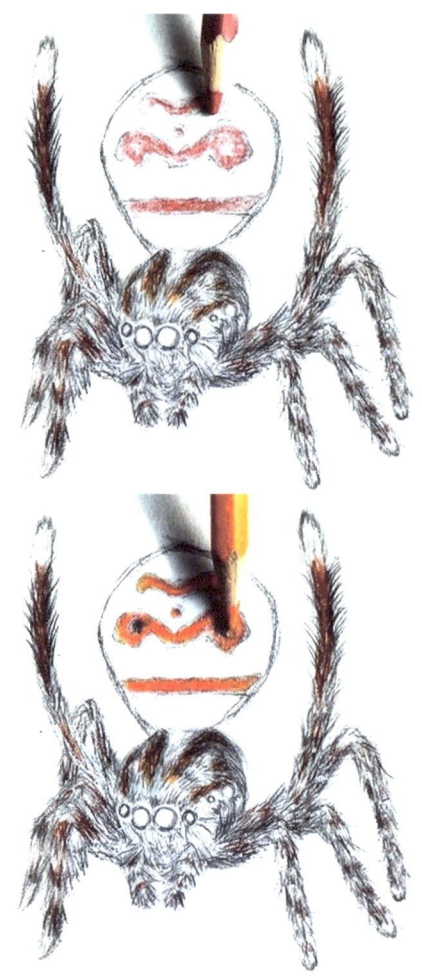

- Define the colors of the abdomen.

The abdominal fan-like embellishment usually contains three to four different colors. The common print that is usually seen contains a red marking that seems to form a smiley face, on a blue surface.

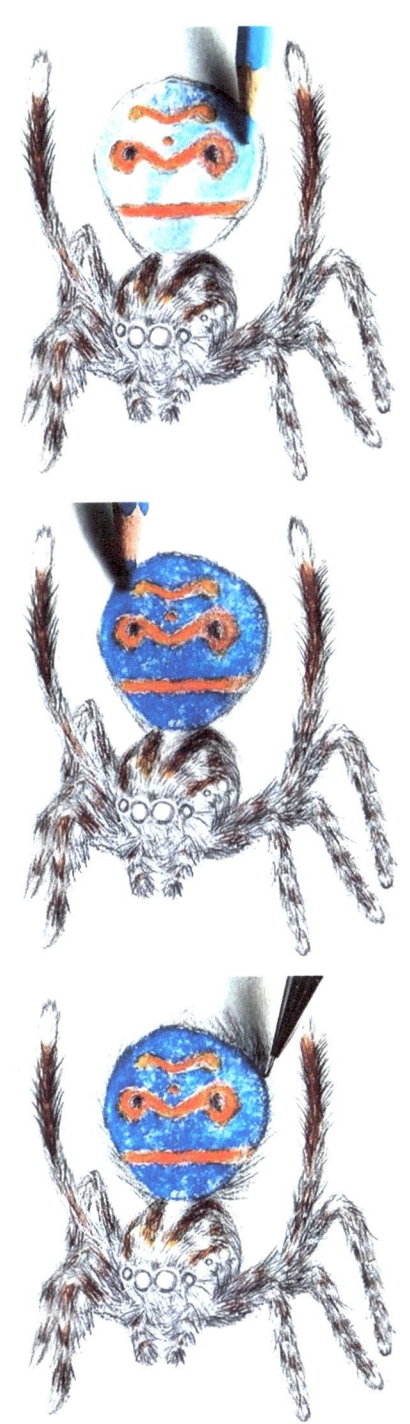

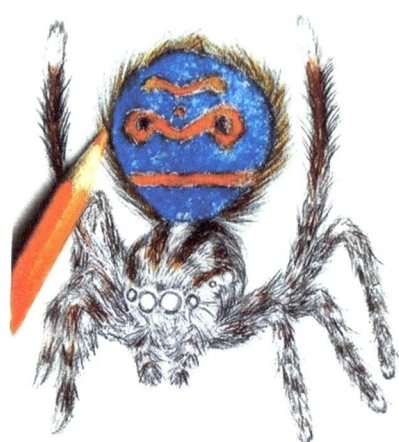

Use scribbling line strokes to create a subtle flaky/scaly texture. For a reddish-orange color of the markings, apply a thin layer of red, and then burnish it with orange. For a bright blue color of the entire surface, use two values of blue. Apply a bright blue color on the nearer side with strong circling line strokes, leaving some subtle portions open, and then fill up the entire surface with a darker blue. When the coloring is done, fill the outer areas with thin long line strokes all heading towards the top.

- Make some final touches.

If an area is too darkened, retrieve the brightness using a kneaded eraser. When the portrayal of its body texture is effectively conveyed, the figure would be defined with the contour hatches and not with a solid and smooth outline. Layering the linear hatches and combining it with texture contour is vital for these kinds of illustrations.

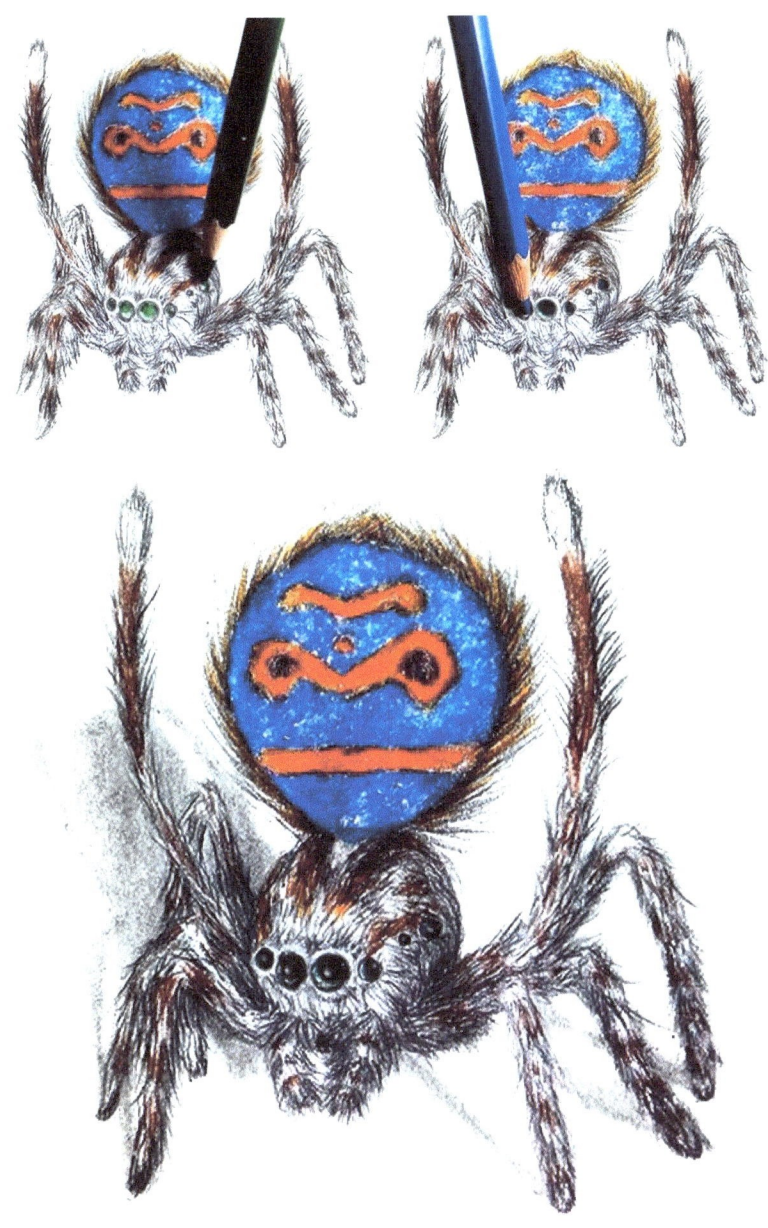

Gasteracantha Arcuata

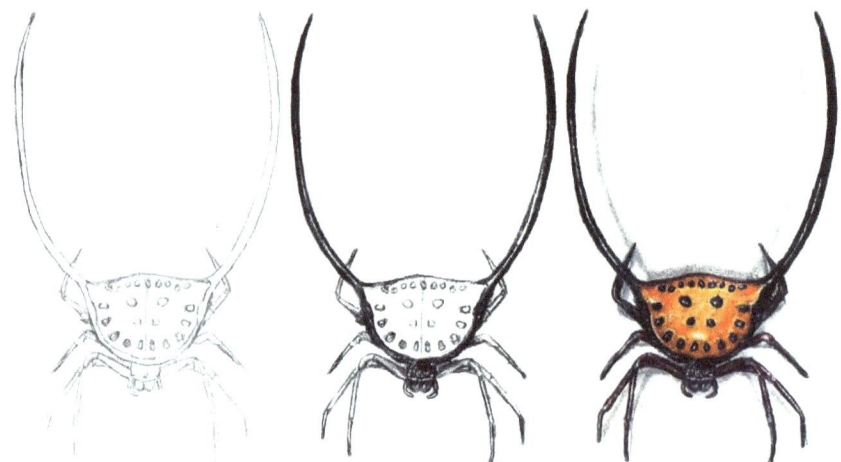

This type of orbweaver is quite rare. The uniqueness of this spider just simply cannot be ignored, even those amongst its certain spider species. Gasteracantha arcuata is a combination of Greek terms, from the word 'gaster' that means belly, 'acantha' that means 'thorn', and 'arcuatus' from the Greek word 'arcus' which means bow or arc. It is also known as the long-horned orbweaver (although, this may also refer to the more common gasteracantha species) or the curved spiny spider. It is also referred as the macracantha arcuata.

The body surface of a gasteracantha arcuata is basically black (excluding the abdomen), but it contains different colors of light and dark values on its limbs. A common color of the limbs is dark-brown/copper to pale black, but there are rare kinds, which has yellow or dark-green color. The limbs could have a single tone or bicolored. The one with green, dark-brown and black, can have two colors or one but of different tone values (usually, black legs can have a brownish or greenish femur). The ones with yellow legs are solid toned, with yellowish-orange tips (tarsus). The shape of its thick abdomen is basically a lower half of a corner-edged circle with curvy sides (can be compared to a crab's), it comes in few different color values of yellow, orange to red, and few kinds have a black or dark grey color. The dorsal side could have a different color from the underside of the abdomen. It has a flat topside (dorsal side) containing black dot marks. The long curving spines on the top corners are usually black, spiking upwards from the base and forming a wide arc. These spines are really long, they have at least three times the length of the base (abdomen) or longer. Like the other gasteracantha spiders, the number and formation of the irregularly shaped black dot marks are uniform. There are 9 small dots on the upper side (if the spider is positioned diagonally in dorsal view) which could sometimes appear as 8 dots or less (if some dots, usually the ones on the middle, are linked together), then 4 bigger dots at the center, and 10 dots at the lower end (slightly bigger than the center dots).

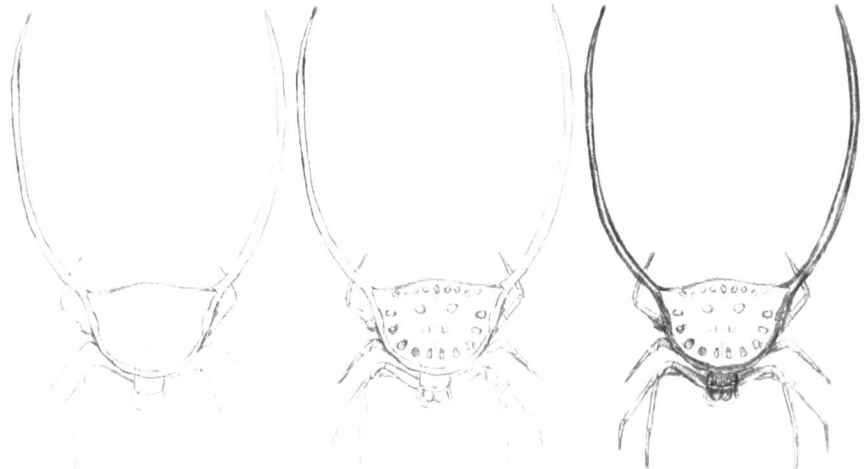

- Establish the shape of the spider.

In dorsal/topside view, the shape of a curvy spine orbweaver is basically a lower half of a thick oval (like a half of a watermelon, cut lengthwise). And at the side edges of the half-oval's top are two very long spines slightly curving inward, extending far from the abdomen. The width of the abdomen is enough to hide the spider's cephalothorax, thus, only the head can be seen if the spider is viewed from the top.

Draw a simple half-oval to establish the size and shape of the spider's abdomen, and then draw a pair of long spikes from the top corners of the oval, with at least three times the length of base. Find the center of the oval and make a reference line, dividing it vertically. Once the center of the oval is established, place the head right below it, and then make the folds and the lengths of the spider's legs using single/stick lines.

Establish the thickness of the limbs and the spines. Draw each limbs as a whole so you can see what portions of each limb overlaps the other. Remember that we are drawing the spider in top view; the folds, thus the portions that subside deeper than the others should be foreshortened (the femur segment of the third pair of legs), although, due to its widely spreading position, it would only require a small amount of foreshortening.

- Define the details of the abdomen.

The abdomen is outlined with a thick margin (excluding the upper side), following/curved with the area of the spines. Establish the black spottings on the abdomen. Use the reference lines to properly position each black spots. Draw nine small irregular circles near the edge of the abdomen's upper outline; with the fifth dot placed at the vertical reference line (excluding this dot, there should be four dots on each side). And near the edge of the abdomen's outline below, draw ten dots that are slightly bigger (or longer) than the set of dots above; each side should have five dots, follow the curving outline of the oval. And then draw four bigger dots at the center, position them in pairs, with the first pair slightly bigger than the pair under it, slightly having a wider gap between.

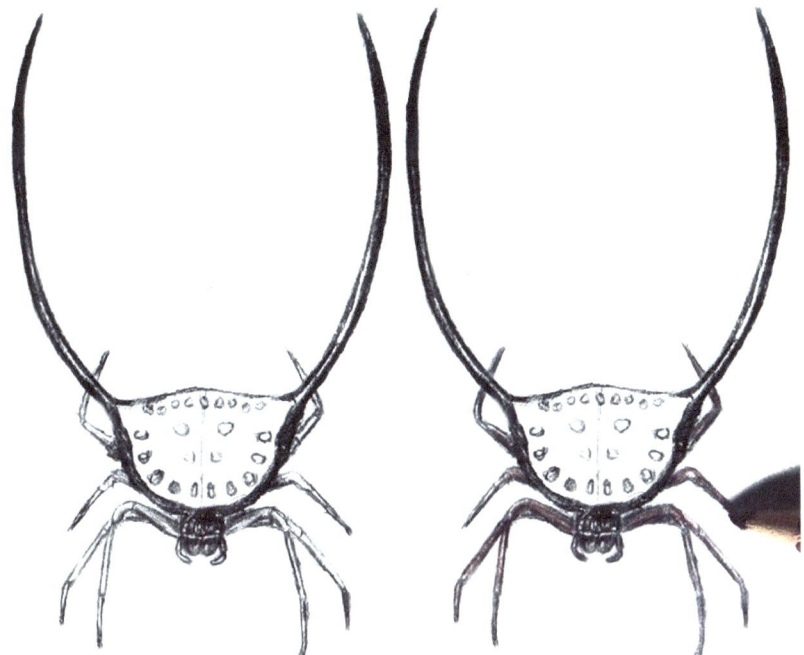

- Apply some shades.

Apply some faint shading on the limbs, with the corners (connecting to the base/body) darker than the other portions of the legs (to convey its downward angle). Apply a dark shading on the margining outline of the abdomen and the long spines, these parts should have the darkest value. Leave a highlight lining at the center portion of the spine to convey its conical dimensions.

- Color the limbs.

Apply a brown color to the limbs (and to the palps). Then re-shade the dark areas once again (overlapping the brown color and blending it with the dark portions). Leave some subtle highlight to the parts should appear nearer (in view), like the knees/patella of the third pair of legs.

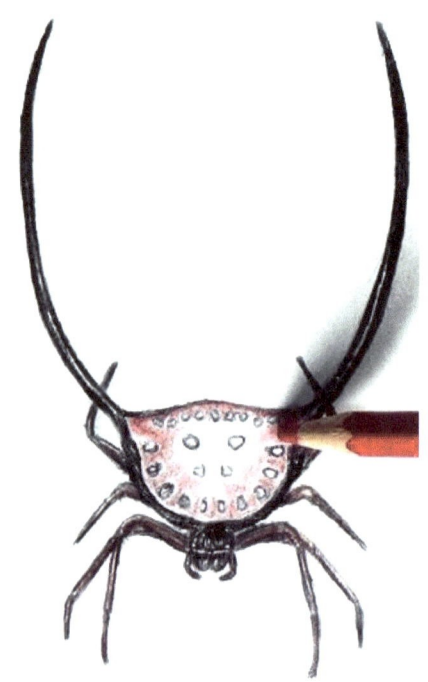

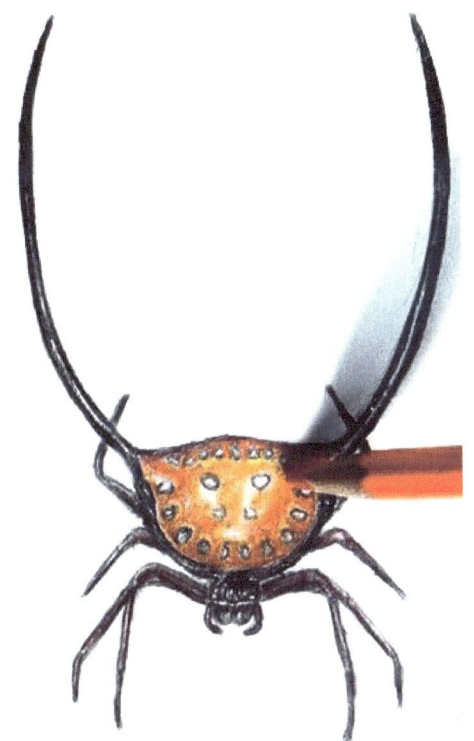

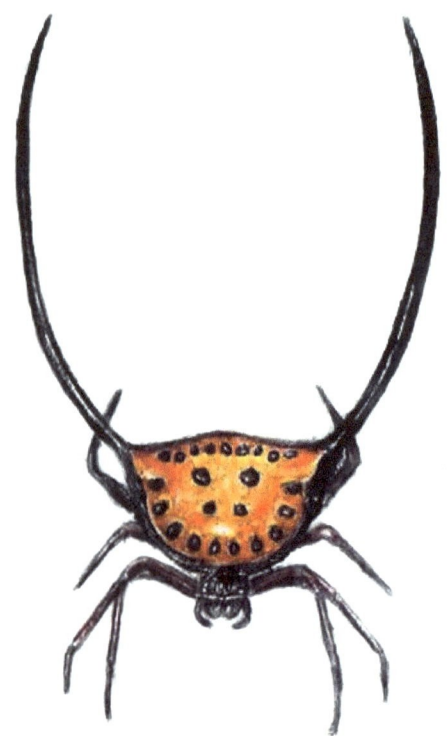

- Color the abdomen.

Start defining the reddish-orange color of the abdomen. Apply some thin layer of red color first, coming from the sides then getting thinner as it reaches the center. Use a light scribbling hand stroke. And then fill the entire area (excluding the spots) with orange.

- Re-shade the darkest areas.

Re-outline the shape of your spider and re-darken the portions that should appear darker. Fill the dots with a dark and heavy shading (leave some small subtle highlight). Then cast a shadow to finalize your drawing.

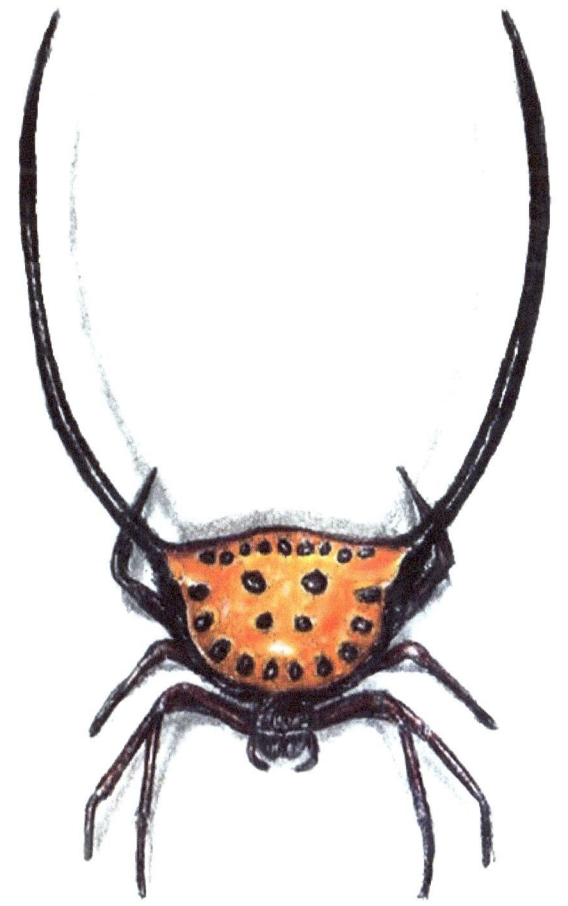

Just like the other orbweavers (and most spider species, for this matter), the females are significantly larger in size compared to males. The size of an adult female ranges from eight to ten millimeter, but if you are going to measure it from spine to spine, it could reach a size of approximately 30 millimeter. The very attractive form of its abdomen also contains black spots (like the other gasteracantha spiders). This unique mutation is probably a way of defense from any potential predators, since the long curvy spines look like thorns (of plants or trees) from afar. The gasteracantha arcuata has a peculiar way of obtaining food, it does not hang at the center of its disk-shaped web when waiting for a prey, but instead, it hides under the leaves then holds a part of its web from there until a prey is caught.

Brazilian Pinkbloom Tarantula

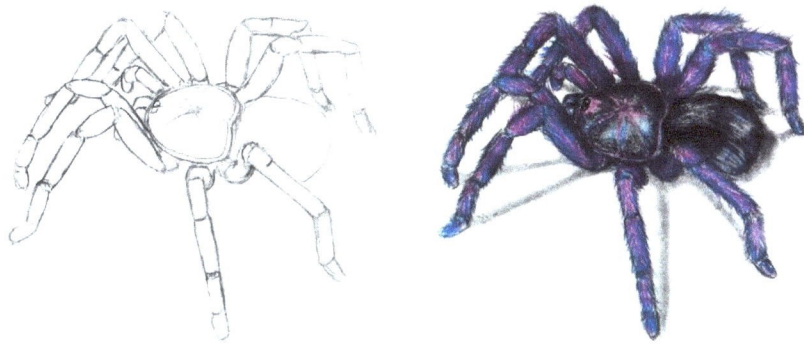

Tarantulas are often collected or kept by arachnid collectors, breeders, or any spider enthusiasts, it's probably due to their size and the stunning colors they possess. And this colorful tarantula is very likely one of the most attractive amongst their kind. The Brazilian pinkbloom tarantula, also called as vitalius wacketi (formerly referred to as pamphobeteus platyomma), is (as the name says) a pink-furred tarantula that can be found on Ecuador and Brazil.

Its body is fairly bulky, the shape is basically a combination of a disk- sphere (but bulky on the dorsal/topside) and oval (abdomen), a common shape and body mass for tarantula species. The brazilian pinkbloom is covered in short fur with vibrant colors, and it is not all pink. The fur covering the black base is basically a combination of strong tone values of pink, purple, and purplish to bright- blue tone. The upper part of the body (cephalothorax) contains a wheel-like print (common in pamphobeteus family) which is an alternating colors of black and pink or purple. The line patterns of purplish pink coming from the center are connected to the margining outline of the carapace/cephalothorax, forming a wheel. The bulky abdomen is more on black-toned than purple/pink, it is covered in long furs spiking upwards (if the spider is positioned vertical with the head at the bottom) towards the upper end. The thick limbs (and also the palp) contain two tones, with the purple or pink blended with black; the colored fur is apparent from coxa to femur, then the pinkish purple color gradually vanishes as it reaches the black-toned tarsus (tip of the limb). The bluish purple color value is subtle on the entire body, as if it creates an iridescent nature to the gradation of the body's coloration.

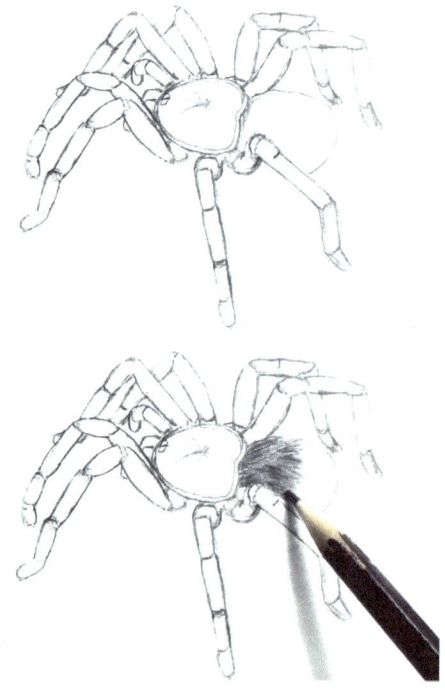

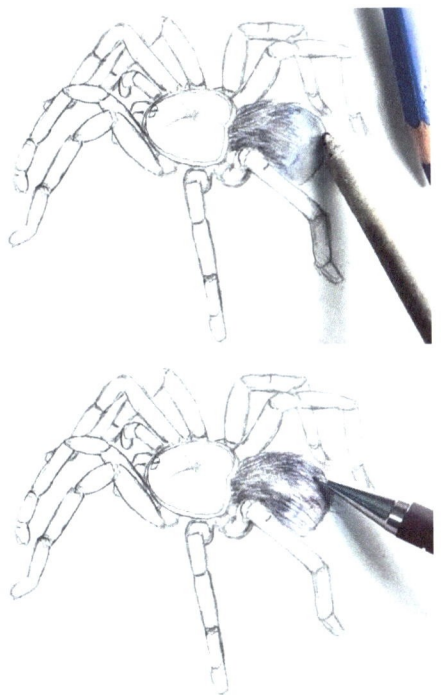

- Make the primary outline.

Establish the shape of the tarantula. The abdomen is basically round, and the semi-heart shaped carapace is almost (just a bit smaller) the same size as the abdomen (based on top view).

Bend/fold the legs gracefully; use single lines first to easily depict how they fold. See what parts of the limbs overlap the other when viewed in a certain angle (in this case, upper side view). Once the limbs are positioned, establish the thickness of each limb. In this angle, the coxa of the nearer legs are partly shown (on second and fourth leg), and the femur of the third leg is foreshortened. The limbs of a tarantula are quite thick (the palps as well); the segments of each leg should be visibly noticeable.

Draw the linings on the carapace. It has four linings, like a cross mark and then overlapped with an X-mark, which intersect at the center of the carapace.

- Convey the hairy texture of the abdomen.

Use thin and long contour hatches to portray the hairy texture of the carapace. Make at least two layers of overlapping (or close together) hatches coming from the side that connects to the upper body. The abdomen has a faint color (use blue) on its lower portion. Apply this color before covering the area further. Smear the color (although, a pencil color can be hardly smudged) to flatten and blur down the coloring.

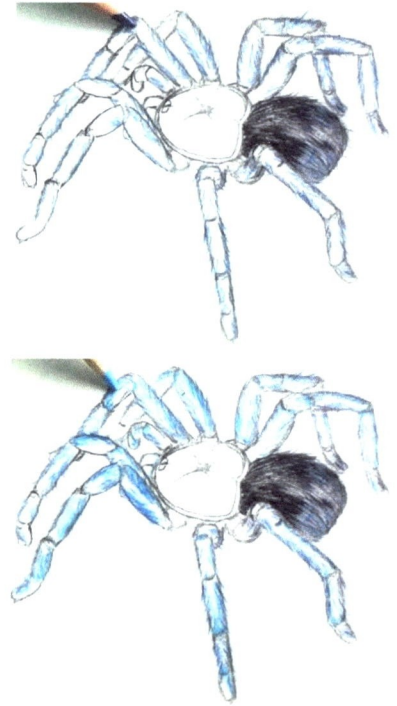

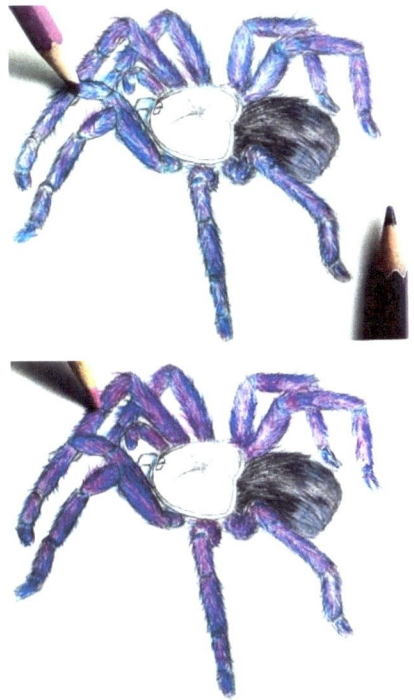

- Apply some blue color for the first color layer.

Start applying the colors of the spider's furry legs. The coloring value of the pinkbloom tarantula is quite tricky, so you have to apply them in several layers to effectively portray the texture while depicting its hue. Apply the same coloring process to the palps.

Start with a blue color. Apply short strokes of blue on the near sides (few at the middle) of the limbs spiking outward from the base/outline. Make some small gaps on each strands to give space for the next color layers.

- Apply another blue color of a brighter value.

Overlap the outlines of the limbs' segments with this color. And in a same manner as you applied the previous blue color, apply another blue tone of a brighter value to the legs. Partially fill the gaps of the darker blue lines (but still leave some spaces), and get nearer to the middle areas of the limbs.

- Apply two different values of purple.

Apply a darker/stronger color value to the limbs. Again, in a same manner, apply the third and fourth colors which are two values of violet (or violet and purple). This time, add more color strands (more than the number of strands of the darker and brighter blue) that could almost fill the areas of the legs.

- Fill the remaining spaces with pink.

For the last color layer, apply strands of pink. Fill what's left of the spaces and overlap the other colors with short line strokes of pink. The center portions of the limbs should have most of the pink value.

If the segment of the limb is positioned downwards (in this case, all of the limbs' segments from patella/knee to tarsus lie downward), then all the short lines/color strands should spike downwards from the base's outline, and vice-versa (like numerous broken 'V's filling the area).

- Color the carapace.

Overlap the linings of the carapace (including the outline) with a thin line of violet, and then overlap it with a thicker line of pink (also apply pink around the dorsal eyes). Put a faint color of blue to the sloping areas of the carapace, and then apply a fairly dark shading (I used a charcoal pencil so I can easily smudge it) then smear it along and across the faint blue tone.

- Add more dark tone.

Darken the areas that should appear darker, such as the foreshortened segments and farther portions of the limbs. Do not use cross hatches, just apply some thin dark strands (like how you did when applying the colors on the limbs) over and over, until the area is dark enough. Also add some few short line strokes (along with the spiking color strands) to add some darker tone and further portray the hairy texture of the limbs.

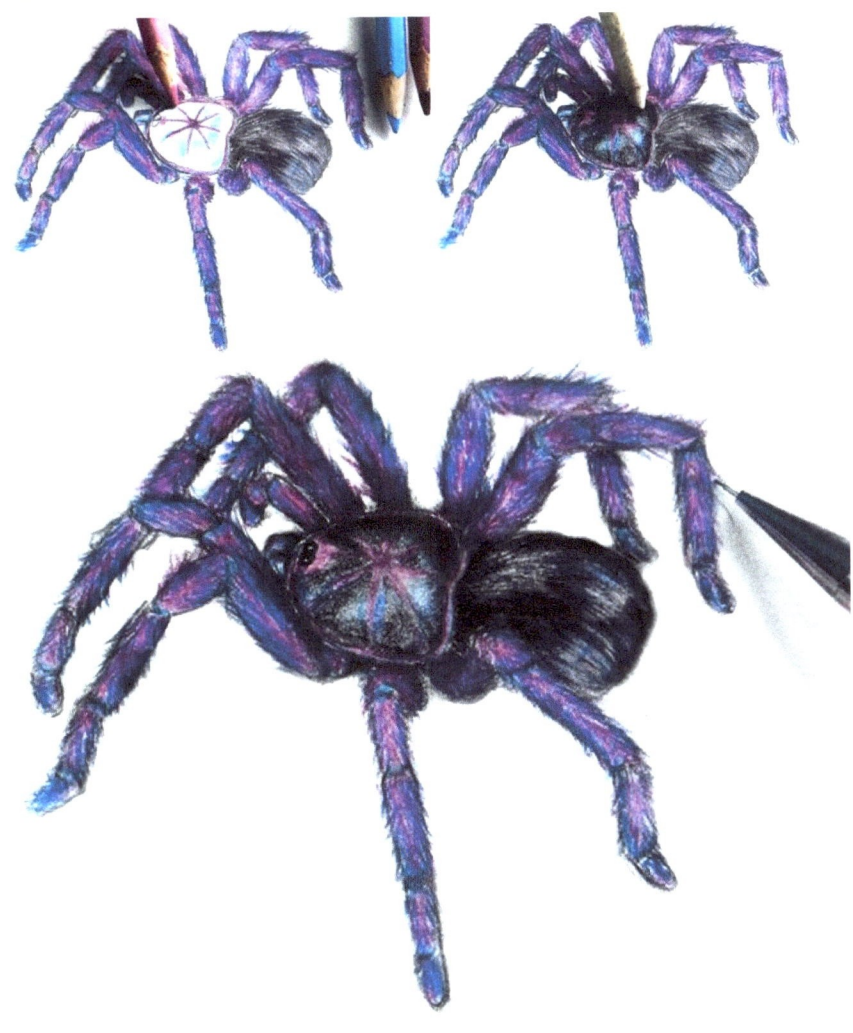

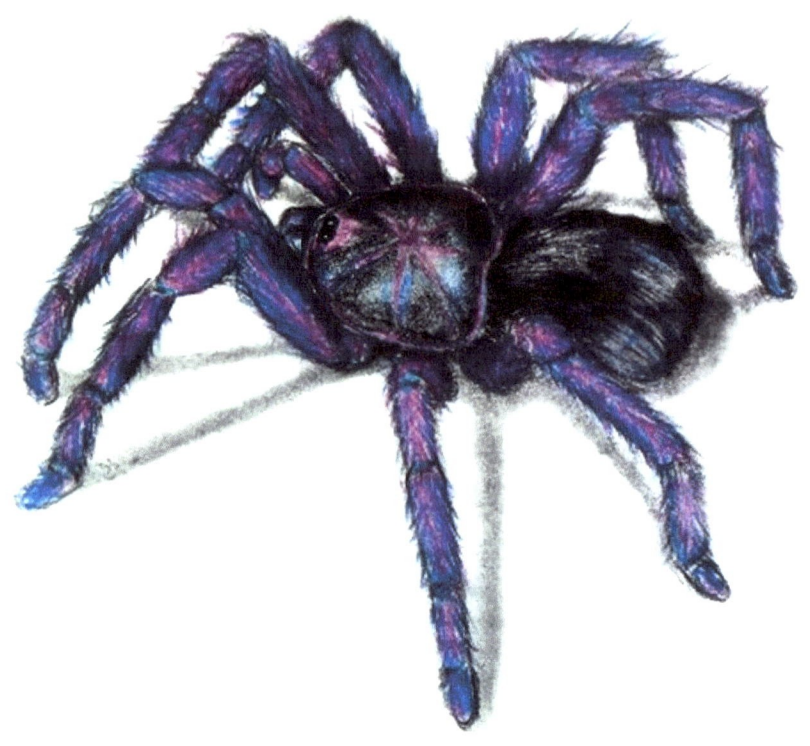

As a known burrower like most other species of its kind, it lives on ground holes for protection against any potential danger. It can grow from nine to eleven centimeters big, with limbs reaching the length of seven to eight inches. Pinkbloom tarantulas are quite aggressive, they will easily respond to any movement with or without any plausible threat against them; they are sensitive to human contact. If within reach, they will flick their hairs which may cause skin irritation. But in spite of this tarantula's known aggressiveness and easily agitated nature, its beauty is worth the risk (and for professional spider handlers, this is not much of an issue), the stunning color hues of this tarantula is just so attractive it almost looks like a toy.

Black Widow

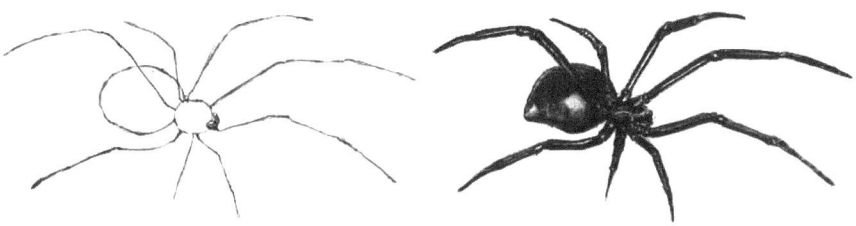

The black widow is one of the most widely known spider, even to those who does not have much interest in the arachnid species. And it is most probably because of the deadly poison it can deliver when it bites. It can be easily recognized by its appearance, the black luster of its body and the signature hourglass print on its bulky spherical abdomen sends forth a frightening vibe that tells you to run away from it as fast as you can. It is often used on movies as a symbol of fear and danger. The venom of this spider is proven harmful; it leads to latrodectism (derived from the scientific name of this spider's family) due to its neurotoxin (latrotoxin). Although, this can be aided through proper medical treatment (if bitten, acquire medical attention immediately).

A widow spider is basically single-toned (excluding the body mark/s), the female is either dark soil-brown or deep copper toned. Most of them are black, all having a shiny texture. There are kinds that are bright -toned and contain more than one body color; the latrodecus geometricus has a pale brown color with few stripes on its limbs. A latrodecus spider of any kind has a small upper body (sephalothorax) and a small head, with a large spherical or oval lower body (abdomen) that is at least three to five times bigger (in mass and shape). They usually have a marking (or markings) on its abdomen, (although few of them do not). The most recognized print on a widow spider's abdomen is the strong toned red or reddish-orange hourglass marking on the underside (ventral side). Some has dot markings lined up vertically around the abdomen, usually with just a pair of irregular spotting, aligned with the hourglass marking. The widow spider latrodectus tredecimguttatus has several red to orange irregular dot marks ringed with yellow, surrounding its entire abdomen ventrally and dorsally.

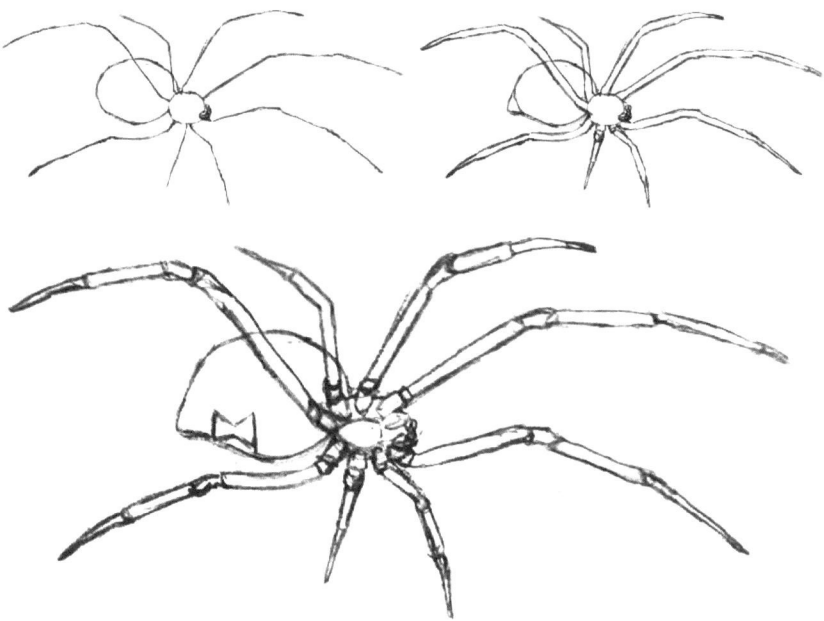

- Construct the primary outline.

It is better to angle this spider in a view where you could see its underside (to expose the hourglass-shaped marking). The abdomen of a black widow is basically spherical if you are going to exclude the spinners; the upper body which is also round is significantly smaller than the abdomen (approximately three times smaller in mass). The limbs are long, and the thickness is fairly proportionate to its body. In an angle (lower side view), the coxa or the part than connects the limbs to the body can be exposed, and also the sternum.

Make two spheres with one (abdomen) having three times the size from the other. Then modify the shape of the bigger sphere; add a slightly protruding portion on the lower side for the spinners. And right above the spinner, draw the hourglass-shaped marking (adjust the shape of the marking with the spider's angled body). Then add the head and the thin and small palps.

Establish the length and thickness of the legs. The second and third pair of legs should be foreshortened (the nearer legs are pointed forward, while the farther ones are point backwards). Once the length and thickness of the limbs are established, define the segments of each leg. And at the center of the upper body, make an outline on the area before the coxa of each limb to establish the sternum.

- Apply the shading.

Put some thick and dark shading on the of the limbs' main outline, and then darken the last segments of the limbs (metatarsus to tarsus). The farther limbs should be darker compared to the limbs that are position nearer. Leave some highlights on each limb to convey its semi-cylindrical shape.

Convey the dimensions of the abdomen's spherical shape by placing different gray tone values. The margining edges should be dark, then gradually getting brighter as it gets to the center.

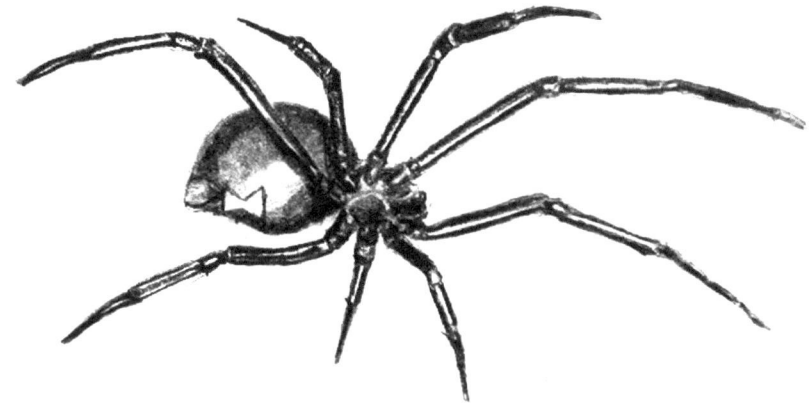

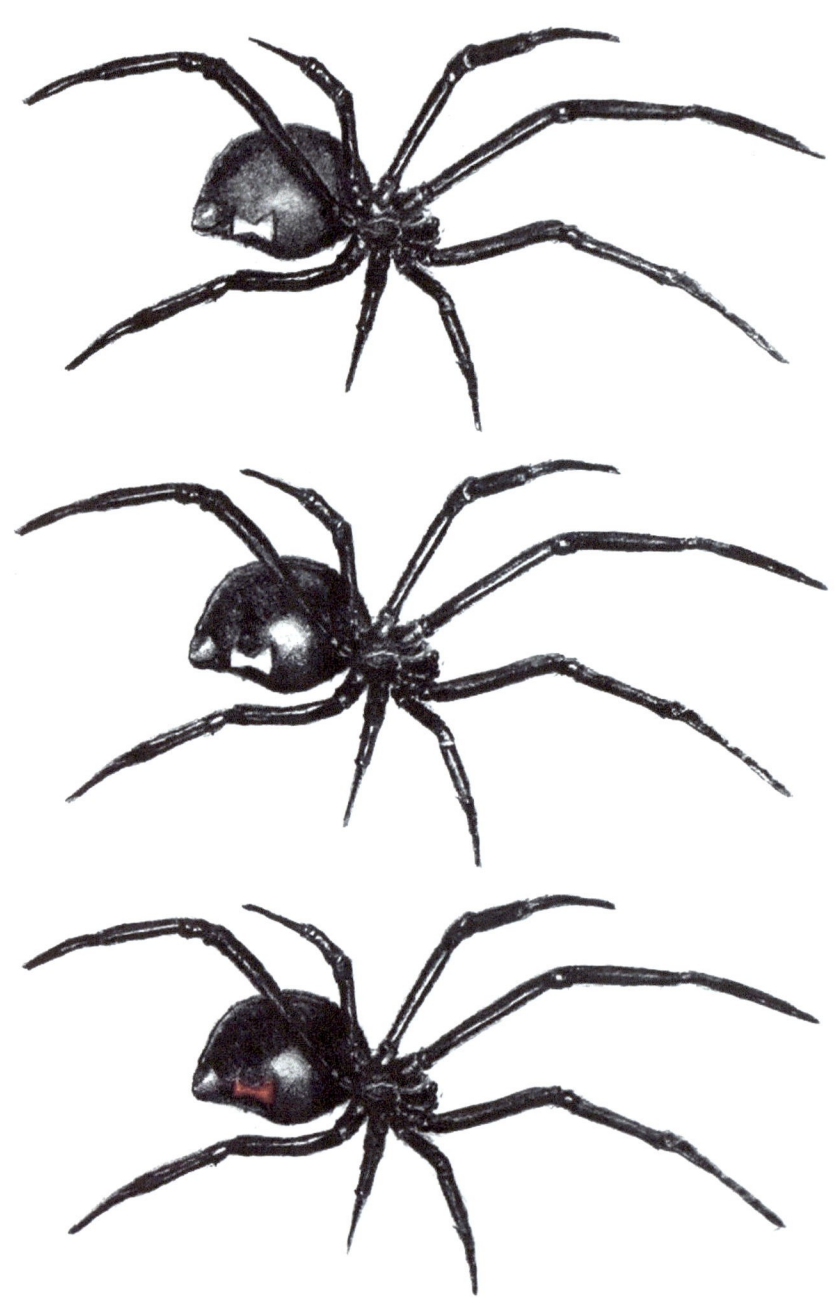

- Smear the shades.

Carefully smear the shade you previously applied. Even out the shading, but keep the highlights on the limbs. Blend down the gradation on the abdomen to smoothen the shades.

- Apply another layer of shading.

Once you already smeared the previous shading, re-darken the areas that should appear darker. Apply another layer of shade using light edgeless strokes on the gray tones, and heavy strokes on the darkest areas. Apply a thin linear contour shading to the darker sides of the abdomen, but leave the brightest portion as is.

Color the red hourglass-shaped marking to finish the drawing. If necessary, re-darken the farther sides of the limbs and the body once more, and retrieve the brightness of the highlights using a kneaded eraser. A black widow spider (as the name says) is solid black, so you need the subtle highlights to portray its contour shape.

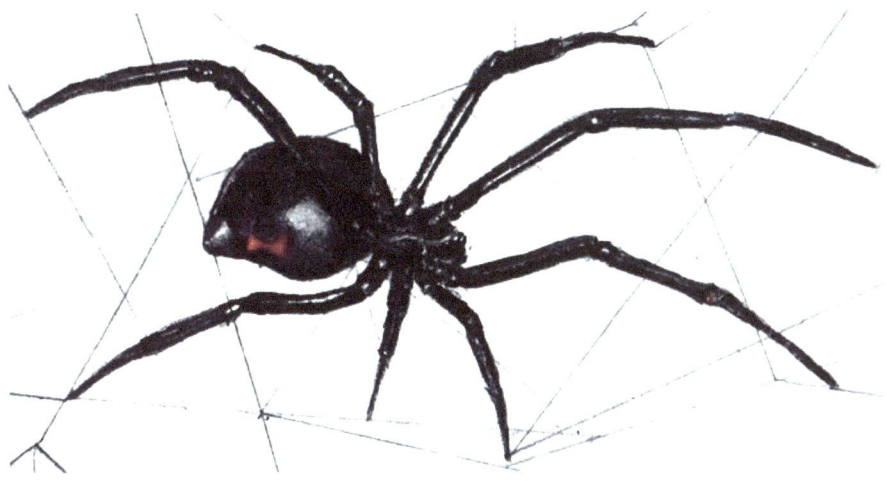

They are referred to as the widow spiders due to their cannibalism behavior towards their mate, as they eat the male latrodectus spider when the mating is finished. But this sexual cannibalism is rare to happen, and they are not the only arachnid species that does this (the female scorpions, for example, are known to consume the male scorpions after mating, which is why the male scorpions instantly flee when the mating is done).

There is more than one type of this spider genus, but the most popular is the latrodectus mactans which is commonly seen in United States, specifically in Southern District. Most of the latrodectus spiders are black, but there are few kinds which have a dark brownish color. The males are significantly smaller, having a lighter color (gray to pale copper brown tone).

Grab the "Drawing Spiders for the Absolute Beginner Vol.2" for more examples.
Thank you for reading.

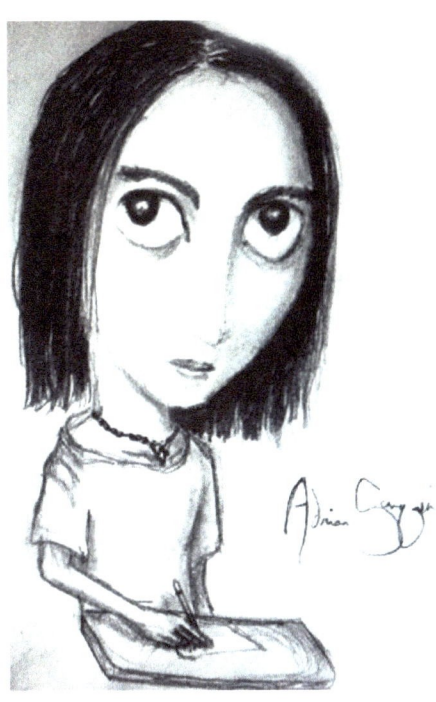

Author Bio

Check out some of my other books:

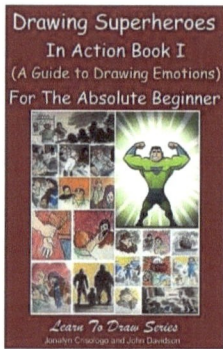

Drawing Superheroes In Action Book I (A Guide to Drawing Emotions) For The Absolute Beginner — Learn To Draw Series — Jonalyn Crisologo and John Davidson

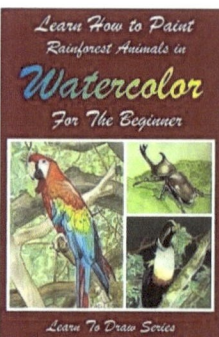

Learn How to Paint Rainforest Animals in Watercolor For The Beginner — Learn To Draw Series — Paolo Lopez de Leon and John Davidson

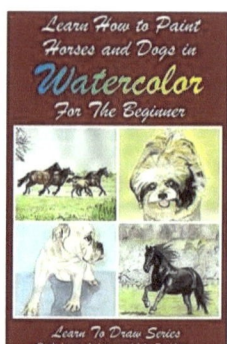

Learn How to Paint Horses and Dogs in Watercolor For The Beginner — Learn To Draw Series — Paolo Lopez de Leon and John Davidson

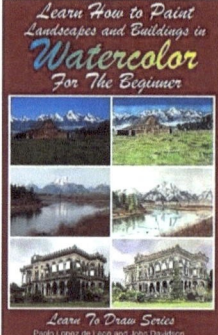

Learn How to Paint Landscapes and Buildings in Watercolor For The Beginner — Learn To Draw Series — Paolo Lopez de Leon and John Davidson

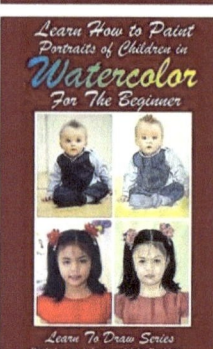

Learn How to Paint Portraits of Children in Watercolor For The Beginner — Learn To Draw Series — Paolo Lopez de Leon and John Davidson

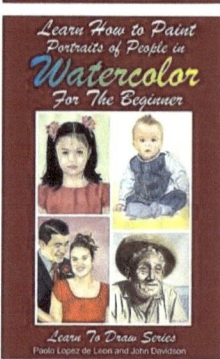

Learn How to Paint Portraits of People in Watercolor For The Beginner — Learn To Draw Series — Paolo Lopez de Leon and John Davidson

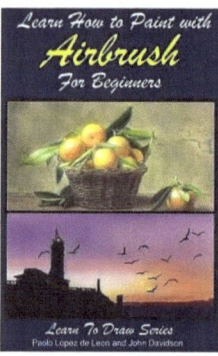

Learn How to Paint with Airbrush For Beginners — Learn To Draw Series — Paolo Lopez de Leon and John Davidson

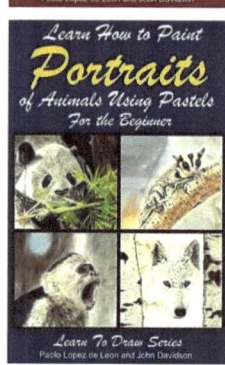

Learn How to Paint Portraits of Animals Using Pastels For the Beginner — Learn To Draw Series — Paolo Lopez de Leon and John Davidson

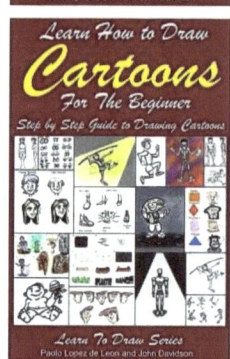

Learn How to Draw Cartoons For The Beginner — Step by Step Guide to Drawing Cartoons — Learn To Draw Series — Paolo Lopez de Leon and John Davidson

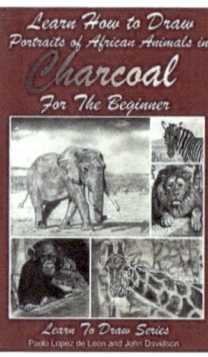

Learn How to Draw Portraits of African Animals in Charcoal For The Beginner — Learn To Draw Series — Paolo Lopez de Leon and John Davidson

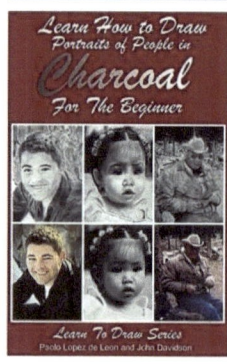

Learn How to Draw Portraits of People in Charcoal For The Beginner — Learn To Draw Series — Paolo Lopez de Leon and John Davidson

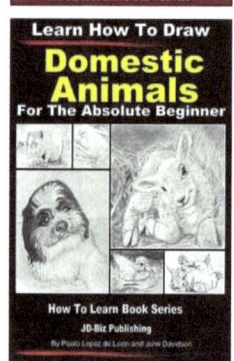

Learn How To Draw Domestic Animals For The Absolute Beginner — How To Learn Book Series — JD-Biz Publishing — By Paolo Lopez de Leon and John Davidson

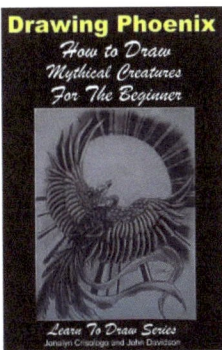

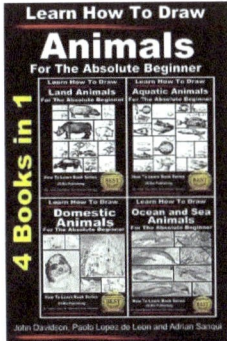

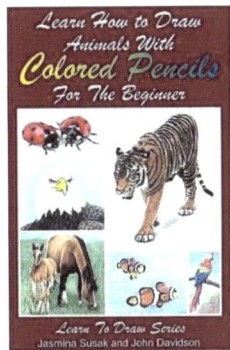

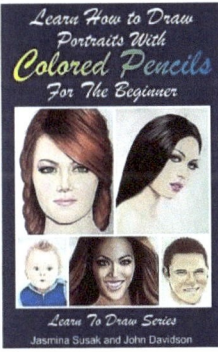

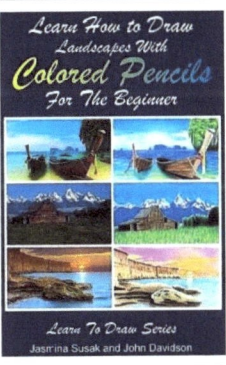

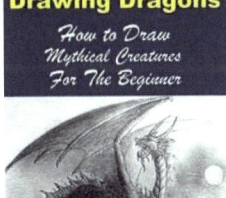

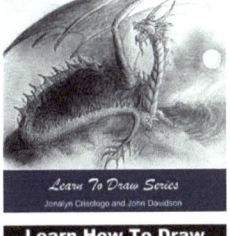

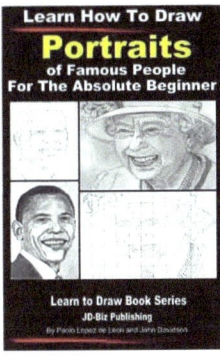

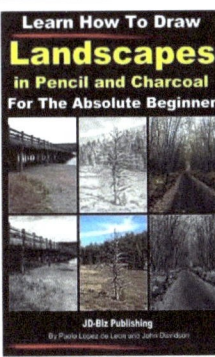

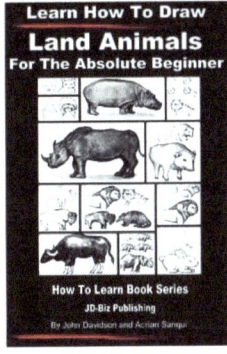

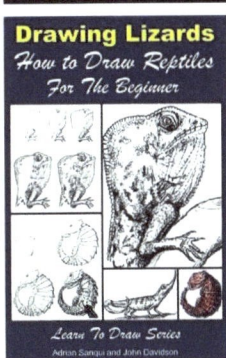

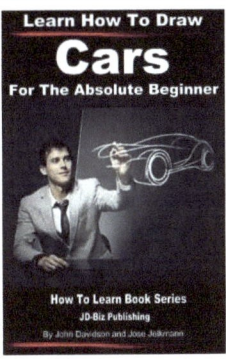

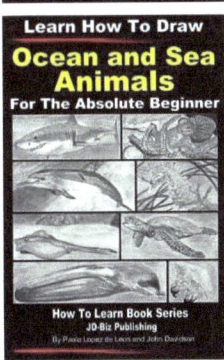

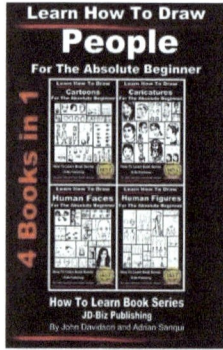

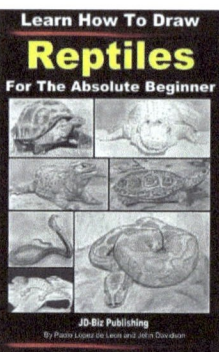

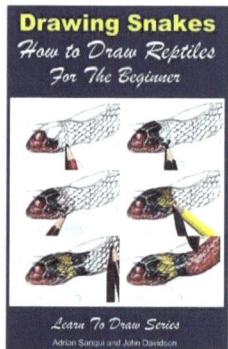

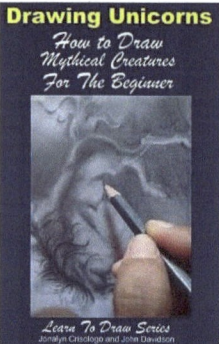

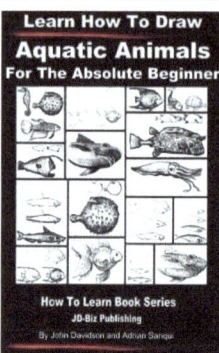

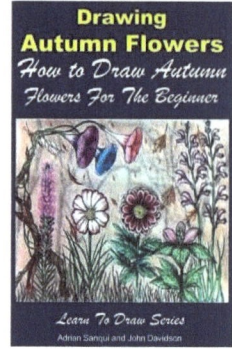

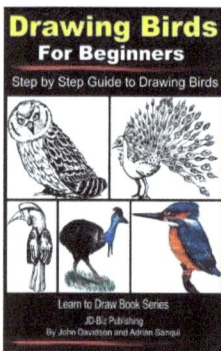

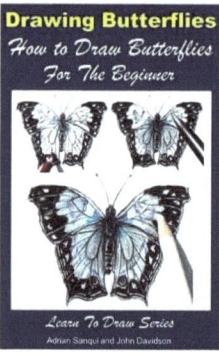

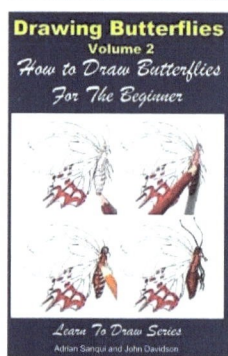

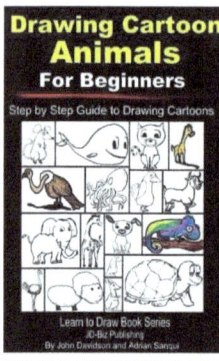

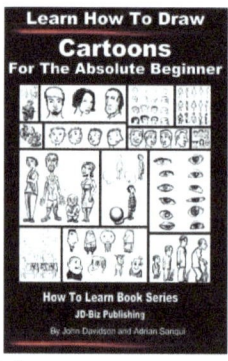

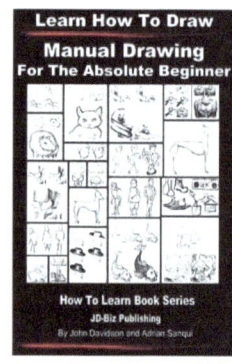

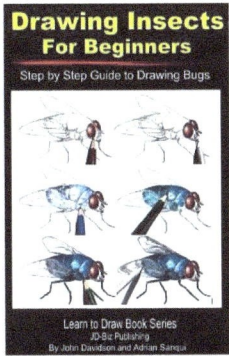

Drawing Insects For Beginners
Step by Step Guide to Drawing Bugs
Learn to Draw Book Series
JD-Biz Publishing
By John Davidson and Adrian Sanqui

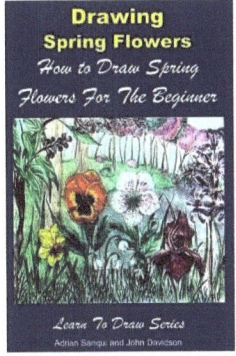

Drawing Spring Flowers
How to Draw Spring Flowers For The Beginner
Learn To Draw Series
Adrian Sanqui and John Davidson

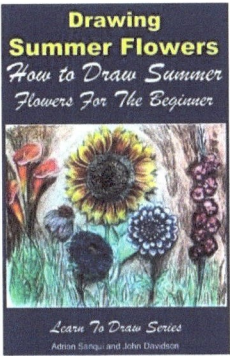

Drawing Summer Flowers
How to Draw Summer Flowers For The Beginner
Learn To Draw Series
Adrian Sanqui and John Davidson

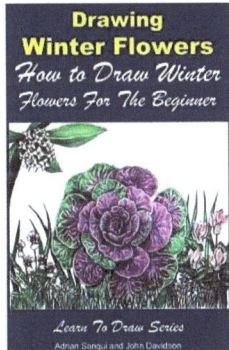

Drawing Winter Flowers
How to Draw Winter Flowers For The Beginner
Learn To Draw Series
Adrian Sanqui and John Davidson

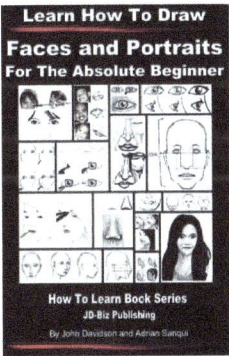

Learn How To Draw Faces and Portraits
For The Absolute Beginner
How To Learn Book Series
JD-Biz Publishing
By John Davidson and Adrian Sanqui

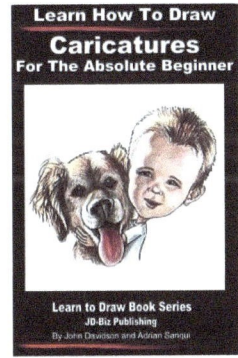

Learn How To Draw Caricatures
For The Absolute Beginner
Learn to Draw Book Series
JD-Biz Publishing
By John Davidson and Adrian Sanqui

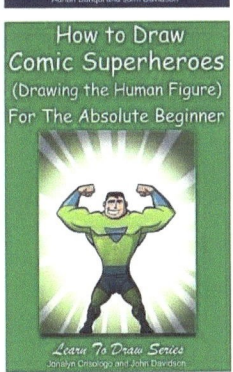

How to Draw Comic Superheroes
(Drawing the Human Figure)
For The Absolute Beginner
Learn To Draw Series
Jonalyn Orisologo and John Davidson

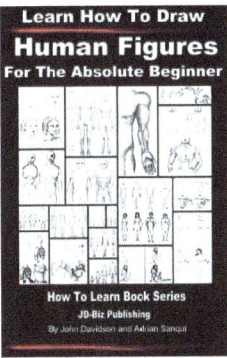

Learn How To Draw Human Figures
For The Absolute Beginner
How To Learn Book Series
JD-Biz Publishing
By John Davidson and Adrian Sanqui

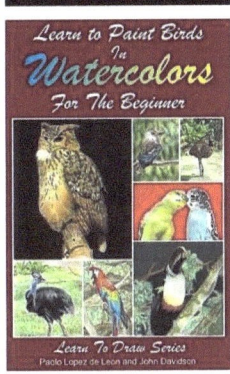

Learn to Paint Birds In Watercolors
For The Beginner
Learn To Draw Series
Paolo Lopez de Leon and John Davidson

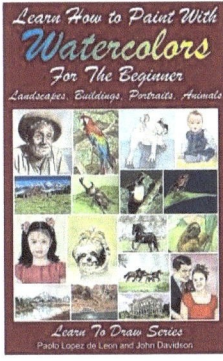

Learn How to Paint With Watercolors
For The Beginner
Landscapes, Buildings, Portraits, Animals
Learn To Draw Series
Paolo Lopez de Leon and John Davidson

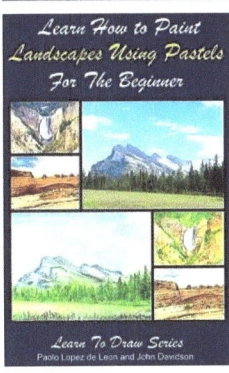

Learn How to Paint Landscapes Using Pastels
For The Beginner
Learn To Draw Series
Paolo Lopez de Leon and John Davidson

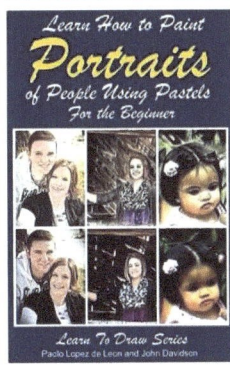

Learn How to Paint Portraits
of People Using Pastels
For the Beginner
Learn To Draw Series
Paolo Lopez de Leon and John Davidson

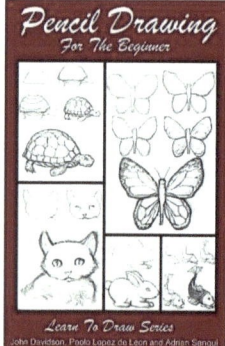

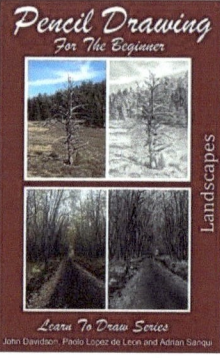

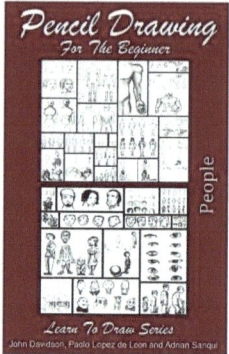

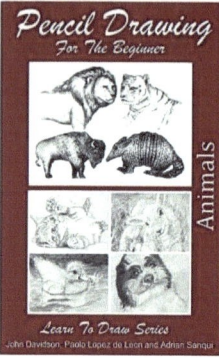

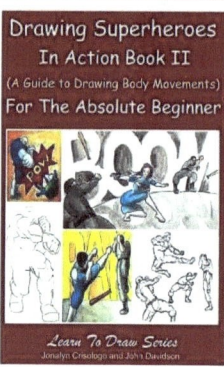

Publisher

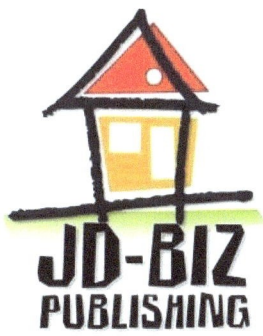

JD-Biz Corp

P O Box 374

Mendon, Utah 84325

http://www.jd-biz.com/

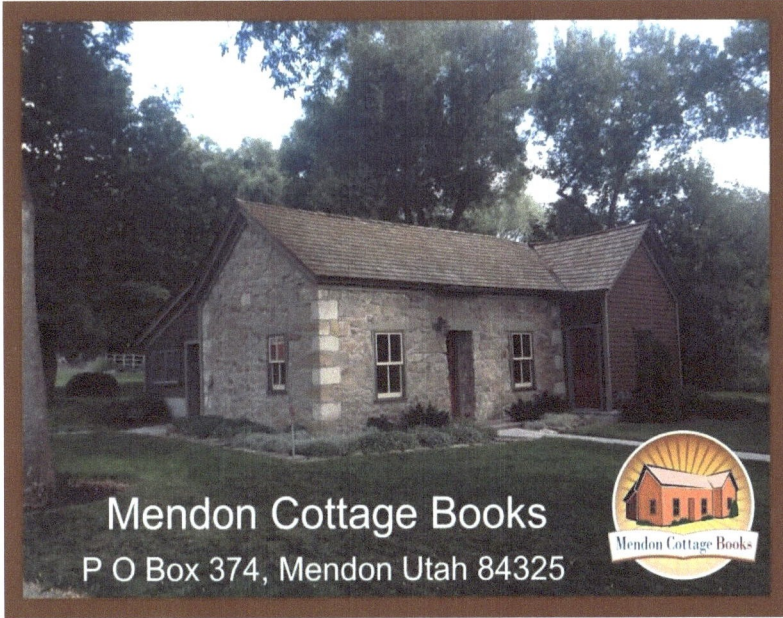

www.ingramcontent.com/pod-product-compliance
Lightning Source LLC
Chambersburg PA
CBHW040858180526
45159CB00001B/462